Teeth

Written by Pete Jenkins
Illustrated by Hazel Quintanilla

SMILE

Rourke
Educational Media
rourkeeducationalmedia.com

Before & After Reading Activities

Teaching Focus:

Teacher-child conversations: Teacher-child conversations play an important role in shaping what children learn. Practice this and see how these conversations help scaffold your student's learning.

Before Reading:

Building Academic Vocabulary and Background Knowledge

Before reading a book, it is important to set the stage for your child or student by using pre-reading strategies. This will help them develop their vocabulary, increase their reading comprehension, and make connections across the curriculum.

1. Read the title and look at the cover. *Let's make predictions about what this book will be about.*
2. Take a picture walk by talking about the pictures/photographs in the book. Implant the vocabulary as you take the picture walk. Be sure to talk about the text features such as headings, the Table of Contents, glossary, bolded words, captions, charts/diagrams, or Index.
3. Have students read the first page of text with you then have students read the remaining text.
4. Strategy Talk – use to assist students while reading.
   - Get your mouth ready
   - Look at the picture
   - Think…does it make sense
   - Think…does it look right
   - Think…does it sound right
   - Chunk it – by looking for a part you know
5. Read it again.

Content Area Vocabulary
Use glossary words in a sentence.

chew
grow
mouth
slimy

After Reading:

Comprehension and Extension Activity

After reading the book, work on the following questions with your child or students in order to check their level of reading comprehension and content mastery.

1. *Why is it important to brush your teeth every day? (Summarize)*
2. *Why do you think everyone's teeth are different? (Asking Questions)*
3. *Name some things your teeth help you do. (Text to self connection)*
4. *What makes your teeth special? (Asking Questions)*

Extension Activity

Make a chart labeling all the days of the week. Now, at the end of each day, write down how many times you brushed your teeth. Next time you go to the dentist, show him or her your chart. Share with them what other things you do to keep your teeth healthy, like eating healthy foods and staying away from sugary drinks. Ask if they can give you more things to do to keep your teeth healthy!

Table of Contents

My Teeth

I see my teeth.

They are in my mouth.

I saw Keli's teeth.

When she brushed them one fell out.

Teeth and What They Do

I see my teeth. They help me when **I** chew.

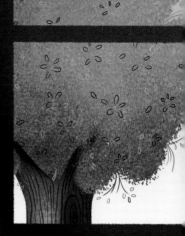

I saw Carly's teeth.

Her juice made them turn blue.

11

My Teeth!

I see my teeth.
I get more as I **grow!**

I saw Alex's teeth.

When she smiles they ALL show.

I see my teeth.

They are white and shiny.

I saw Johnny's teeth.

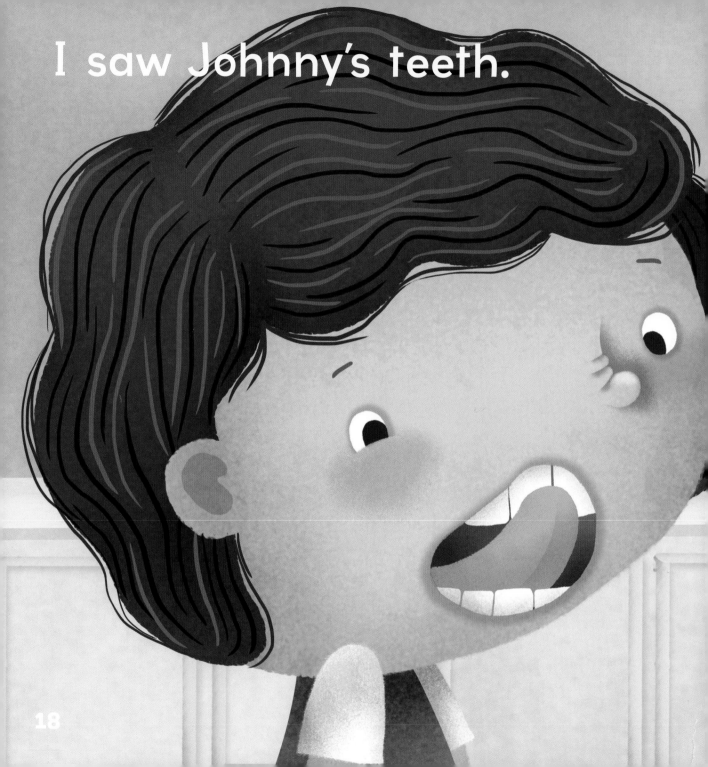

He said that his feel **slimy**.

19

I see my teeth. They make my smile look pretty.

I love my teeth!

Picture Glossary

 **chew** (choo): When you chew, you grind food between your teeth.

 **grow** (groh): When something grows, it gets bigger in size.

 **mouth** (mouth): Your mouth is the opening in your face that helps you eat, breathe, and speak.

 **slimy** (SLIMY): When something is slimy, it is slippery or dirty.

About the Author

Pete Jenkins always tries to take care of his teeth. His teeth were not always nice and straight and he even had to wear braces when he was younger. He didn't mind, though. He thought they were cool. He enjoys using his teeth to eat healthy foods and the occasional not so healthy foods as well.

Meet The Author!
www.meetREMauthors.com

Library of Congress PCN Data

Teeth/ Pete Jenkins
(I See, I Saw)
ISBN 978-1-68342-313-3 (hard cover)
ISBN 978-1-68342-409-3 (soft cover)
ISBN 978-1-68342-479-6 (e-Book)
Library of Congress Control Number: 2017931163

Rourke Educational Media
Printed in the United States of America,
North Mankato, Minnesota

Edited by: Keli Sipperley
Cover and interior illustrations by: Hazel Quintanilla
Page layout by: Kathy Walsh